I0425320

REACH WITH PASSION, AND YOU SHALL RECEIVE

THE WORLD NEEDS YOU, NOW SHOW IT WHY

LEAD THE WAY, YOU ARE THE LIGHT

WHEN YOU HAVE THE WILL, YOU WILL FIND THE WAY

EVERY HURDLE WILL BRING YOU CLOSER TO YOUR GOAL

VISION YOUR GOAL, THEN WALK THAT PATH

IN THIS LIFE YOU CAN HAVE IT ALL

WE ARE WHO WE MAKE US TO BE

YOU ARE IN CONT OF YOUR REACTIONS, SO MAKE THEM POSITIVE

POWER COMES FROM THE MIND, SO BUILD A STRONG ONE

THINK! WHO YOU WANT TO BE

THE BEST TIME TO BE SUCCESSFUL WAS 20 YEARS AGO. THE SECOND BEST TIME IS NOW

AN AUTOMATED LIFE IS NOT WORTH LIVING

POSITIVE MENTAL ATTITUDE

TIME IS SHORT, WALK YOUR OWN PATH

BE THE BEST, YOU KNOW YOU CAN

I DRIVE MY VEHICLE

IN ORDER TO CLIMB, YOU MUST FIRST PUT DOWN YOUR LUGGAGE

TAKE CONTROL OF THIS DAY, YOU KNOW YOU CAN

MOTIVATION IS ALL AROUND YOU, JUST LOOK AND YOU WILL FIND

IF YOU HEAR A VOICE FROM WITHIN YOU SAY "YOU CAN'T ," PROVE YOU CAN AND THAT VOICE WILL BE SILENCED

IF YOU DON'T ASK, YOU WONT GET, IF YOU DON'T SEARCH, YOU WONT FIND

DREAM THE LIFE, AND LIVE THE DREAM

FOLLOW YOUR HEART, NOT YOUR EYES

_____

_____

_____

_____

_____

_____

_____

_____

_____

_____

_____

_____

_____

_____

_____

_____

_____

_____

_____

_____

BELIEVE YOU CAN AND YOU WILL FIND THE WAY

FEAR IS THE WALL BETWEEN SUCCESS

YOU ARE SURROUNDED BY OPPORTUNITIES

IT CANT HAPPEN IF YOU DON'T TRY

THERE IS BEAUTY IN EVERYTHING, LOOK

ACT NOW, MAKE YESTERDAY CREATIVE AND LIVE TOMORROWS DREAM

KNOW YOURSELF

www.ingramcontent.com/pod-product-compliance
Lightning Source LLC
Chambersburg PA
CBHW081542280526
45788CB00010B/3325